A FEW WORDS
FROM SOME OF OUR CLIENTS

"Using the Online Proposal System we've won far more business than we would have otherwise. Being able to see when and how long someone's read our proposals for is vital. I can now follow up at the perfect time and win the business. Genius!"

Bradley Jones, Founder of Printergage
www.printergage.com

"Communicating effectively with my readers, prospects and clients is the most important part of my business. Keeping all this information up-to-date in separate systems is a nightmare. In my Business Automation System, it's all in one place and I can email from a beautifully branded template, to any segment of my database."

Tim Coe, Author of 'your Utterly Seductive Proposal' and Managing Director of myUSP
www.myusp.biz

"Advantix has been a great help in building a reliable, straightforward fully customised software system allowing us more time to focus on the core activities of our business. Advantix always delivers and the on-going service has been exemplary. If you are a company looking to improve your workflow, processes and efficiency I would urge you to talk to Adam of Advantix"

Robert Baggs, Tax Consultant at iTax Consulting
www.itaxconsulting.com

"My Business Automation System allows me and my staff to keep in touch with prospects and clients that would otherwise have slipped into thin air. The value of simply following up effectively has paid for the system already."

       Tom Aitken, Managing Director of Enhance Services
                www.enhanceservices.co.uk

"Our Business Automation System has revolutionised the way we think of our leads, prospects and clients now. It's so easy to see exactly what's going on with any contact at a second's notice."

          Matt Hunt, Managing Director of OLOVES
                    www.oloves.com

"Advantix really encouraged us to be involved throughout all stages of development of our system, and Adam's innovative ideas and conceptual thinking brought a very welcome element to the process."

       Claire Tyne, Office Manager at MAA Architects
               www.maa-architects.com

COCKTAILS & PALM TREES

Cocktails & Palm Trees copyright © 2014 Adam Hempenstall

The moral rights of the author have been asserted.

All rights reserved. No part of this publication may be reproduced, distributed, or transmitted in any form or by any means, including photocopying, recording, or other electronic or mechanical methods, without the prior written permission of the publisher, except in the case of brief quotations embodied in critical reviews and certain other non-commercial uses permitted by copyright law. For permission requests, write to the publisher, addressed "Attention: Permissions Coordinator," at the email address below.

Cover design by Zakk Williams at www.flipthebirdmedia.com

Self Published by Lulu.com

All enquiries to adam@advantixgroup.com

First published 2014

COCKTAILS & PALM TREES

THE STEP-BY-STEP GUIDE TO
AUTOMATING YOUR BUSINESS

ADAM HEMPENSTALL

SPECIAL THANKS TO...

Sabrina, for being a legendary business partner, friend and sounding board.

Zakk at flipthebirdmedia.com for doing an indescribably brilliant job of the cover artwork.

And all our clients who part with their hard earned money every month and continually put trust in our ideas.

I love you all.

TABLE OF CONTENTS

PART 1: RE-THINKING WORK

1:	Adopting the Broker Business Model	17
2:	Logistics of Having a Mobile Business	22

PART 2: THE WALKTHROUGH

3:	Organising Your Enquiries, Clients and Contacts	29
4:	Connecting Your Website to Your CRM	35
5:	Email Marketing in the Year We Actually Live In	47
6:	Selling Like a Champion	56
7:	Simplifying Your Work Day	72
8:	Automate Your Business Finances	81

PART 3: DESIGNING YOUR NEW LIFE

9:	Making the Transition	91
10:	Getting Your Team On-Board	105
11:	The Big Jump and the £1,000 Reward	111

IS THIS BOOK FOR YOU?

There are some businesses and people that this book isn't suitable for. I don't mean, read it but it won't work; I'm actively telling you not to read it because you'll get a taste of the life you could have, but with your current business, you'll be powerless to do anything about it. If the following applies to you, just give the book to someone else or be prepared to change your business entirely:

- You are about to retire and have no idea how to use computers.
- Your business involves lots of red tape. For instance, Mortgage Brokers often require a physical signature on application forms and there's no way around it.
- You are too large a company to make changes quickly.
- You have a majority business partner who hates making changes.

Conversely, if you've had enough of working long hours and the business seems to be doing the same it always has, then is now not the time to change?

Adam Hempenstall

Founder of Advantix

COCKTAILS & PALM TREES

INTRO
WHY READ THIS BOOK?

MY STORY
AND WHY YOU NEED THIS BOOK

For those of you who have read my first book, Automate Your Business, you already know this story, but for those that are new to our business, let me fill you in.

Something that always fascinated me as I grew into an adult was this idea that you could call any company and by just giving them an account number, they could tell almost everything about you. As I started thinking more about business, I couldn't help but ask the question, "Why don't small businesses have this stuff?"

From the beginning of 2002 right up to 2009, I built a web design agency which built lead generating websites for small businesses. More and more though, we'd be asked questions like "You know the bit where I can log in and edit my website, can you build something like that so I can manage my clients?" As time went on we shifted more and more into building business software.

Before long it was more or less all we did. A random 3am conversation with my good friend Tim Coe cemented the idea that we were going to close the web business and become a software company. We'd been building software to automate businesses for years, so why not call them Business Automation Systems?

For next 6 years we focused solely on building the best systems possible, innovating where others had ignored and steamrolling while others were chilling. In doing so, we produced life changing results for our clients.

I had two life goals. One was to build my own house from scratch. I hope to start this in a few years. The second was to have the money and time freedom to travel anywhere in the world at a moment's notice. I'm sitting here in my hotel room in Milan finishing this book without any worries that the business is being destroyed back home because it's right here with me. I'm my own walking case study.

Now I've accomplished the dream of being able to travel when and where I like with my business, I've realised my third goal: To help as many people achieve whatever freedom, fun and adventure based dreams they have using our tools.

This book will help you figure out what your goals and dreams are, then structure your business around living your own ideal lifestyle.

WHAT YOU'LL GET OUT OF THIS
IF YOU FOLLOW THE INSTRUCTIONS

This book is a passport. It's your key to running a business that gives you freedom, fun and adventure.

Whether you want to earn more money, work less, or simply reduce the paperwork, this book can help you do all those things. If you want to, you could run your business from a five star beach resort in Thailand and travel to the far corners of the Earth, or you could stay in the office but work a 20-hour week instead. If that's too far out, how about working a normal 40-hour week, having a healthy relationship (not ruined by late nights and working weekends), spending time with your kids and the admin handles itself?

This guide will provide you with all of the information, ideas and tools to make it all happen; you just need to be prepared to follow it. You will come up with hundreds of excuses along the way but I want you to ignore them as they're mostly invalid. If you think of something that isn't in the book, there will be an 'Ask Adam' link on our website where you can type your question and I'll answer it. I don't want you to have any excuses at all.

Whatever your goal is, it starts with you. Your staff aren't suddenly going to spring into action and make you a billionaire overnight. You are the leader, the conductor and the captain. Once you reach the end of this book and I have you "bought in" to the idea of having a mobile business, you need to get the "buy in" of the rest of your team.

Once you explain to the people involved in your business that the idea isn't to sidestep issues or put them out of a job, but rather get their perspective, you'll find everyone chips in to help. This starts a chain reaction to create an automated business which gives everyone in the team more freedom. It's a beautiful thing that I've seen happen many times before.

Let's get into it.

WHY
COCKTAILS & PALM TREES

I don't think many people ever truly work out why they wake up in the morning. I'm hardly a philosopher, but I know that I wanted to see as much of the world as I could. I wanted not only the money to do it but the time freedom too.

I know the websites of many business software systems promise a wonderful lifestyle because of their benefits, yet the owners mostly have tons of staff and all work crazy hours. Nice advert! The best example of an automated business I can give you is to answer your call 3 minutes before I'm about to jump off a mountain attached to a paraglider or reply to your email while I'm on the beach in Spain. Our support team are around to deal with the day-to-day operations while I'm free to do whatever I like. You should strive to do the same.

You have to work out what your "cocktails and palm trees" dream is. It could be spending more time with your family, waking up late and going to bed late, or simply working less because you don't actually enjoy going to work. These are all valid and that's the reason why this book is structured the way it is. Everyone that comes on board with us goes through the same process regardless of their situation, yet all their goals are different. Ultimately, you need to be out of the business, not in it. For some small businesses, this is a long weekend project, for others it's a carefully crafted 12 month plan. Whatever the situation, the process is the same.

This book is in 3 sections:

1. Re-Thinking Work
This section will bring you up to speed with the tools, systems, skills and mindsets you'll need to bring your business into the 21st century.

2. The Walkthrough
A step by step guide on creating incredible marketing, world class proposals and following up like a champion. You'll be guided through a process to simplify your workflow and reduce your finance admin down to just a few hours a month.

3. Designing Your New Life
Taking everything you've learned and created, and re-designing your business to suit your life, not the other way round. Will you take me up on my challenge?

PART 1
RE-THINKING WORK

Chapter 1

Adopting The Broker Business Model

WHY DO THE WORK
WHEN YOU DON'T HAVE TO?

There are many different business models but the one I want to explore today and the ultimate business model is the "broker" model. This is where you don't involve yourself with the production element of your business, but you control the marketing and sales. This allows you to focus your efforts on the money and not worry yourself with the drama of actually producing the goods, sending them out etc. An example:

There's a chap in Worthing, UK who I did some work for years ago. He was a steel fabricator, we'll call him James. He made handrails for elderly people to fix to the bathroom wall to stop them falling over and knocking themselves out. He had a cool little business but what was amazing was that despite his product being aimed at 70 year old men and women, he was making 18-20 sales a day online! He was selling these handrails delivered for £99 and could make them for about £30. Tidy profit of £1,180 a day! Unfortunately his factory, 3 staff, office, materials, insurances and delivery costs sucked up a good chunk of that profit.

Here's the funny thing though, he had a friend in the same business whose marketing sucked but he took care of the overflow production work for James. He charged him £50 all in, per handrail. I said to James that he was mad and should just give all the work to his mate, shut his factory down and work wherever he wanted. He couldn't bring himself to take the leap. Such a shame.

The real value to your clients is well presented marketing, a simple ordering process and great customer service. All those things slip when you need to get your hands dirty 8 hours a day. Your product or service could ultimately be made by anyone so long as it looks like it's come from you.

For you, it doesn't need to be as drastic as firing all your staff and shutting your factory down. Maybe that was a big ask, but it could be as simple as stepping back from production yourself and insisting on a set process. Perhaps cutting down the product range and producing less products but more efficiently. I've written at great length about this in my first book 'Automate Your Business'. You can order your copy at www.advantixgroup.com/automate-your-business.

Here are a couple of short examples of regular, every day businesses operating under the 'broker' business model.

Tom Aitken of Enhance Services - A training company in Sussex, UK
www.EnhanceServices.co.uk
Tom brilliantly designed his business processes with the broker model in mind. His business is running training courses like First Aid in Schools, Colleges and Universities, but his profession is marketing and outsourcing, and he does a superb job of it. His job is simply to get the bookings and book the trainer - that's it. He's known for providing regular work to trainers so he is inundated with people who want to deliver courses for his business. Naturally, it was easy to automate the processes Tom had created.

Tim Coe's previous business, Hands-On Properties based in Hampshire, UK

www.Hands-OnProperties.com

I still remain amazed at how genius Tim was to do what he did with Hands-On Properties. Not only did he find a product that everyone wanted (reducing the Stamp Duty when you buy a house by 50%), but he managed to avoid all the legalities and responsibility. To make matters even better he didn't even have to do anything. He'd just generate the enquiry and pass it on to his partner, iTax Consulting who are also clients of ours. They would do all the complicated paperwork, assume all the risk then pay Tim each time there was a successful sale. Absolute genius. Unfortunately, the Government have made it so difficult to sell the service now it's not worth the effort but it was great while it lasted. Tim now runs myUSP, a marketing agency dedicated to making your business stand out. His new business website is www.myusp.biz

Bradley Jones of Printergage based in Sussex, UK

www.Printergage.com

Printergage is a joint project between our business and 3 others. It's an online print shop with the software to process the orders. It was developed by us but Bradley's business essentially just works on the marketing, gets the clients, and then hands them over to us to set up. We have processes internally to outsource this, meaning it's scalable.

Are you seeing a pattern here? Neither Tom, Tim nor Bradley have scalability issues, meaning for every client they sign up, there's no additional hassle, just revenue and profit. How can you switch your business up to just focus on the marketing and sales, then leave the production to someone else or outsource it entirely? Without covering every single eventuality, it's near impossible for me to tell you how you should do it. After all, I don't know you or your business yet.

If you do want my input or advice you can contact me (details at the back of the book) or go to:
www.advantixgroup.com/askadam and I'll get back to you with my thoughts.

Chapter 2

Logistics Of Having A Mobile Business

HOW TO TRAVEL THE WORLD
AND BE AT YOUR DESK

So many business owners that I speak to have an excuse as to why their business can't be automated. Often though, the changes don't have to be massive and in reality, most people don't even notice or care, yet you benefit massively.

The first thing to realise is, nothing is permanent. It's not necessarily like you're looking to move somewhere like Miami forever. It's important to set your business up to be mobile even if you stay in the same place all year round. One reason being that it increases the value of your business should you ever wish to sell it. That said, you'll still want to attend to some of the major logistical changes.

Your Main Company Phone Number

Most businesses these days have an 0845 or an 0800 number which forwards to a fixed line. If this is the case for you then you won't have to change your number or do anything in addition if you don't want to. In your marketing, you can promote the 0800 number and offer a 'local' alternative for the people calling from mobiles.

If you don't have an 0800 or 0845 number, just get yourself a Skype In number and have that be your default number. More and more small businesses these days are using mobile phones as the primary phone to make calls from and don't want to pay a premium for an 0845 call, and 0800 numbers aren't free from mobiles. With Skype In numbers, if you're based in London, you can have an 0208 number, Brighton you can have an 01273 number etc. Even better, let's say you wanted a London presence, but lived elsewhere, just get a London Skype In number and away you go.

Just set the Skype forwarding to your mobile or landline and you're ready to go. If you are abroad and working, you can switch off the forwarding and take the calls on your laptop without paying mobile charges.

Your Business Address

Depending on the type of business you're in, you might be more reliant on a physical address, but most businesses can operate quite happily without one. If you want to give the impression of a bigger company you can always use a mailing address. We moved out of our office nearly 3 years ago but kept it as a mailing address and I've had 2 items of post in all that time.

I appreciate that in some instances, you need a proper address and that's fine but do it out of necessity, not thinking you need to. That's actually a common theme throughout this book and the concept of Business Automation in general. Do things out of necessity, not because you think you should.

Meetings

Accept this fact as truth: People want meetings with you more than is necessary. That said, start saying no to meetings more often, especially when a sale isn't on the cards. For us, every major client gets a quarterly meeting if it involves less than a 1 hour drive. I'll meet potential clients but usually only if a demo has been done over the phone, they like what we do and they know the price, or have a ballpark figure if it's some custom development. This way the meetings are never pointless.

Meetings to update people should never happen, there's simply no need. Don't meet people to go through anything - don't be a glorified note taker for them. The exception to this would be a massive multi-year project where these kinds of things are expected.

Try to avoid having an 'open door' or a 'drop in' policy if you can help it. It lets other people dictate how you're spending your time which will almost always cause stress at some point.

Keeping Tabs On Your Business

It's all well and good sitting in a hammock in Fiji with a cocktail taking calls, but if you can't keep track of the day-to-day running of the business, you're going to be back on that plane pretty quickly!

The only way you can do this, without the whole operation collapsing, is running your business using web-based software. Gone are the days when you would need to ring the office and try to get hold of someone who could give you a full update. All you need is an internet connection, and you'll have all the information you need at your fingertips.

WHAT SYSTEM SHOULD I USE?

There aren't many systems on the market that allow you to automate your entire business. What we are giving away to readers of this book is a 90 day free trial of your very own Business Automation System. In addition to that, we'll set it up for you in advance so you really can use it for 3 months uninterrupted to work out if it's for you.

I truly believe that we have the only workable solution for small businesses who want to automate. This is my second book on the subject and I've been selling these systems, innovating in this area for nearly 10 years, and I've yet to come across anything that compares.

In short, we'll give you the system and all the help you need to get going. If you find it's worth the money, then maybe you can consider becoming a client.

STARTING YOUR TRIAL OF THE BUSINESS AUTOMATION SYSTEM

At this point, I'm hoping you're at least on-board with the idea of automating your business. Now we're going to switch gears, dust off the laptop and set about actually doing it. We've got everything sorted for you, all you'll need to do is fill in the blanks, follow the instructions and you'll be away!

If you are reading this book for information but aren't really interested in actually automating your business right now, or maybe the timing isn't right, just pause here and come back to it when you're ready.

If you're ready to roll then you'll need a computer and to fill in a trial request at:
http://www.advantixgroup.com/cocktailsandpalmtrees/trial

We'll create your account within 24 hours and will contact you to arrange an initial discussion. Unlike most business software where you sign up and are left to figure it out yourself, that's not how we work. We will have a discussion and we'll set everything up for you. There's of course no pressure to continue using it.

If you don't want to use our system, don't worry, you're not entirely on your own. I'll say now though that I make no mention of other CRM systems or quoting systems because if I thought they were good, I'd use them myself and wouldn't have spent 6 years of my life building our own. You will however build up knowledge of the kind of system that you could use and can do your own Google searches to find something appropriate.

PART 2
THE WALKTHROUGH

Chapter 3

Organising Your Enquiries, Clients and Contacts

GATHERING YOUR DATA

As your business has been built over the years your data could be anything from neatly organised in spreadsheets to scattered all over the place looking like you printed it all out and launched it into the ceiling fan. Your job right now is to try and pull it all in into one place.

If your current situation means you maybe have clients over here, enquiries on sheets of paper, and the rest in your brain. Now is a good time to take some time to get it all in one place and know, going forward that it's all organised. This is the hardest task. Everything else is easy in comparison.

SEGMENTING YOUR ENQUIRIES, CLIENTS AND CONTACTS

I would recommend splitting your contacts up into 3 groups:

- Enquiries
- Clients
- General Contacts

Doing it like this keeps it simple and in order. Typically you'll keep your general contacts on your mobile phone, clients are often in a spreadsheet and enquiries will probably be in a separate spreadsheet or on bits of paper. If you have a daunting number of contacts then split this job up into 3 different tasks and attack each segment one at a time. Use the same spreadsheet template for enquiries, clients and general contacts. This helps to standardise the data you have collected.

IMPORTING EVERYTHING

If you have another CRM system that you're going to use, you should be able to import this data yourself without too much trouble.

> **IF YOU ARE USING THE TRIAL**
>
> We have a template you can download to start populating your client data. Once it's ready to go, just email support@advantixgroup.com and we'll import it for you:
> http://www.advantixgroup.com/downloads/client-spreadsheet

As always, if you have any questions, just jump on over to the 'Ask Adam' section of our website and fire away with your question, or send a text to 07793 823301.

http://www.advantixgroup.com/askadam

LEAD
SOURCES

Back in the old days, you'd run ads in 20 magazines every year with no real idea if any of them would work. It would take years of trial and error to see if stopping any particular ad had any impact on sales. Of course you could always ask the potential client "So how did you hear of us?" but most people can't remember what they had for dinner last night never mind which magazine they tore your ad from.

With that said, it's so vital in this day and age to understand exactly where your clients come from. Let's say you're using Google Adwords and spending £500 a month driving traffic to your website with no response, you'd be wasting £6,000 a year so obviously you'd re-think it and try again.

The benefit is you don't need to wait until the end of the year in order to cancel the failing ad, you just switch it off if it's not working, which heavily reduces the amount of money wasted. That's the power of modern day digital marketing. Almost every major platform allows you to track the effectiveness of your ad spend.

This doesn't mean that if you use print ads you can't track the results. Tom Aitken at Enhance Services runs a number of ads in magazines but has given each ad a different phone number and web address. He can then log into the control panel and look at the number of calls each number gets in order to track the effectiveness. The web addresses forward to his website but in the process track the number of visitors the ads get. Any enquiries that he gets are then passed directly into his Business Automation System with a note for the advert it came from. This smart use of technology enables Tom and many others who do a similar thing to make smart marketing decisions.

On the flip side, there might be some advertising or marketing that you're running which is producing epic results, which you have the option to increase. If you can see that a free listing in a directory or a cheap ad in a magazine is producing sales and you can increase the size of it for example, then it would be worth you doing exactly that. Without tracking this information you're flying blind and will waste considerable amounts of money.

In the next chapter, we'll talk about starting this tracking process from when the enquiry comes through on your website.

CATEGORISING SALES ENQUIRIES

Not all sales enquiries are generated equal. A referral from a long-term client is better than a tyre kicker after the best price who has called 7 other companies. Naturally, you'll know which are the likely buyers so it's important to categorise these enquiries. I've personally always used a traffic light system - green for good, yellow for maybe, red for unlikely. Others have used 123 or ABC. In the Business Automation System we've used traffic lights because it has a visual element too for instant recognition.

It's important to do this because when it comes to re-engaging these contacts with email marketing campaigns, the 'green' ones are likely to be more receptive to relationship building, whereas the 'red' guys are likely to be more receptive to a strong offer to grab their attention. Of course it all comes down to how you choose to grade them, but having a criteria that you operate by means that you can market to them more effectively going forward.

Whether it's the Business Automation System you use or something else, make sure this is something that is built in and allows you to email them directly from the system. It's one of the easiest ways of generating sales from the existing enquiries you have. We'll cover this in detail in Chapter 5.

Chapter 4

Connecting Your Website With Your CRM

BRINGING IT
FULL CIRCLE

Most business do their marketing in a straight line. They get an enquiry and it either converts into a sale or it fails.

WEBSITE ENQUIRY **SALE**

This is a flawed plan. Not only are details not tracked, but following up effectively and efficiently is a near impossible task. Without your enquiries automatically being passed into your Business Automation System or CRM, it's likely your conversion rate is far lower than it should be. In order to bring it up, you need to know at which stage of your sales process your prospects are dropping off.

For instance if you are getting the enquiries but not sending that many proposals, it's likely your initial follow up is weak. If you're putting lots of proposals out there but not getting many sales, this is probably due to your proposal not demonstrating the value, or you're marketing to people who can't afford your product.

Without tracking each stage, you are completely flying blind and have no idea which area of the process to improve. The best way to start the process is by having your enquiries go directly from your website straight into your system.

Think about it as a closed loop rather than a line:
This cycle repeats itself indefinitely either by re-selling the same product, or by up-selling them the next item in the series.

In this example, it's dots 7 and 8 we're concerned about. When you start re-marketing to your existing clients again and driving them back to your website for round 2 in a well thought out and meaningful way, that's when you see serious results.

AN EXAMPLE
USING A PRINTING COMPANY

Take a printer for instance. Their cost of winning business is so high, they must take advantage of the customers they do win, yet they never seem to. I've used many printers in the past and honestly, Lulu (http://www.advantixgroup.com/links/lulu), the company we use to print these books, are the best by far at re-marketing to me. They'll send me an offer for another round of books roughly in accordance with how many I've ordered. They make it quick and easy by telling me all my artwork and book PDF is already uploaded, I just need to choose how many I want. They sweeten the deal with a coupon for 25% off usually and a big obvious call to action. Brilliant!

I've never been re-marketed to for a repeat order of business cards. I frequently order brochures from printed.com yet I never get an email saying "Do you want anymore of those brochures, you must have gone through them all by now. Here's 10% off if you order today". How hard is that really? How effective do you think it would be if you emailed all your customers a TARGETED, informal and friendly offer with an easy call to action? I'm predicting a pretty solid response.

Not re-marketing usually comes down to a lack of technology and systems. If you think that's where you're falling down then hopefully you'll have plenty of ideas and solutions by the end of this book.

AN INTRODUCTION
TO LANDING PAGES

If you've been reading anything about marketing online in the last 6-8 years you'll know exactly what a Landing Page is, but for clarity's sake here's a reasonable definition from Wikipedia.

"A single web page that appears in response to an online advertisement. The landing page will usually display directed sales copy that is a logical extension of the advertisement, search result or link."

In other words, it's where you'll send your visitors from either a Pay Per Click ad or an email marketing campaign. The idea is to ensure that there's complete continuity when going from your ad/email to your landing page. There are a few things to consider, to do this easily:

- **Branding** - make sure it's prominent on both the marketing material and landing page.
- **Imagery** - If you have a picture of an apple on your email, get the apple on the landing page too. Aim for instant recognition.
- **Headline** - Reference the ad. It acts as a subtle indication that the reader is in the right place.

Here's a terrible example:

A screenshot of the email:

Chris Howard
1 August 2014 11:24 more...
To: Adam Hempenstall
IF YOU OPEN ONLY ONE EMAIL FROM ME THIS YEAR - Make it this one - SEE WHY!

CREATING WEALTH FROM THE INSIDE OUT

Hi Adam

Chris Howard here, **and I have an opportunity for you that WILL ABSOLUTELY BLOW YOUR MIND!**

As you may or may not know, I've spent the last couple of years in the rainforest jungle paradise of Ubud, Bali. **And now I have headed home to the U.S. and bringing everything in tighter to home after almost over two decades of being on the road full time.**

As such, Rock House is having a wrap-up of major trainings that our U.S. based company will be holding in Bali throughout the month of September. **As we don't plan to run these trainings in Bali or Australasia anytime other than THIS round** in the immediate future, I am going to give you an opportunity unlike any other opportunity EVER OFFERED BEFORE – To **TAKE YOUR TRAINING TO THE HIGHEST LEVEL- IN PARADISE and FAST for a FRACTION of the COST!**

This is TRULY the OPPORTUNITY OF A LIFETIME!

Even if you have attended these trainings before you may very well want to take the leap and either re-take them, or have the opportunity to **take some of them directly from the source – with me personally** – right now for pennies on the dollar!

SO.....
WE'RE HAVING A REVOLUTIONARY TRAINING CELEBRATION IN THE RAINFOREST JUNGLE PARADISE OF BALI AND YOU'RE INVITED!

We have the following four trainings:

- TLCC: Transformational Leader and Coach Certification
(Become certified as Transformational Leader, Transformational Coach, Practitioner of Transformational NLP, Ericksonian Hypnotist) - 7days

- MTLCC: Master Transformational Leader and Coach Certification
(Become certified as a Master Transformational Leader, Master Transformational Coach, Master Practitioner of Transformational NLP, Master Hypnotist – **Walk out with the ability to deliver $2,500 Personal Breakthrough Sessions** – *You could pay for the entire trip and training pack with only 2 Clients!) - 7 days*

A screenshot of the landing page it links to:

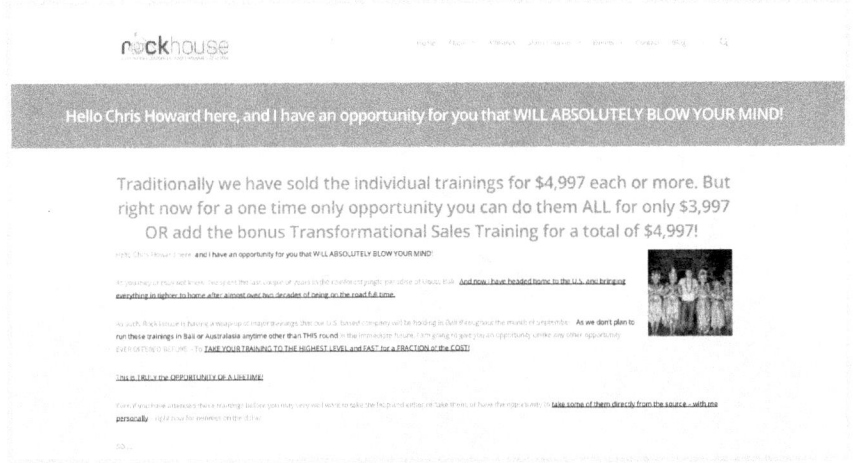

This is fundamentally terrible. The headline in the email has nothing to do with the headline on the landing page. There's no matching imagery at all, just random photos of the trainer with foreign dancers. The 'call to action' in the email is so far down the page it got cut off, but mentions the discount. The branding is consistent at least, but looks incredibly overbearing, and almost childish.

Here's a great example:

Screenshot of the email:

Hey Ads,

I just wanted to share with you the latest blog post. Let me know what you think.

How to Create an Instagram Shop in Five Easy Steps

Instagram is often overlooked by many for promoting their products and services, especially by agents of influence and small business owners. However, there's a way to garner much needed attention, but more importantly sales by using it in a very specific way.

Click here to find out now to boost your sales by using Instagram now.

Enjoy!

Ben Angel

PS: If you haven't signed up for the new 30 Day Business Turnaround Program, you can do so here.

Screenshot of the landing page it links to:

What's he done right here? Firstly, he's used the same imagery so you instantly know you're in the right place. The headline is the same, and again, instantly recognisable. The only thing not overly prominent in the traditional way is his branding but saying that, the emails come from Ben Angel, and right there on the right is a picture of him and his name.

This is easily repeatable. In order to set yourself up with a website that allows you to create these landing pages, I recommend you find yourself a web developer that runs a proper business. Cheap freelancers are great but can often be unreliable. Just make sure they want regular work and are superb at Wordpress.

We recommend you contact Owen who runs our web division:

Contact: Owen Carr

Email: owen@advantixgroup.com

TRACKING THE SUCCESS OF YOUR MARKETING

Once you start creating different landing pages with different offers, you'll want to start tracking which ads/email campaigns are working. The way most marketers do this is what's called a 'tracking code'. Don't worry if this is going over your head slightly, it won't be anything you are actually doing yourself. We'll liaise with your web developer and help them set it up or if you use Owen, he'll know exactly what to do.

"Why use a tracking code?"

Imagine you're running 20 ads on Facebook Advertising, 12 on LinkedIn Advertising and 56 on Google Adwords but it's all for the same promotion and therefore going to the same landing page. Let's assume you start getting 10 sales enquiries a day flying into your inbox and system, how do you know whether it's Facebook, LinkedIn or Google that's producing the results? Without a tracking code, you won't. This can lead to the biggest waste in profits ever - paying for advertising that isn't producing results.

You need to be working towards having the knowledge to make smart marketing decisions. Blindly running ads is not the way to do it. How to do this is pretty simple in reality.

Here's a normal link:
http://www.advantixgroup.com/trial

Here's one with a tracking code:
http://www.advantixgroup.com/trial?src=FB-EMMS-Blue

For each advert, you simply tweak the code at the end (everything after the = sign) to let you know what it is. For complex marketing campaigns, it's worth getting a spreadsheet and simply using numbers followed by the actual ad. For small campaigns, that's not necessary in my opinion. Looking at this code, I can tell it's from Facebook for a start because it has 'FB' at the beginning, EMMS means 'Email Marketing System' so I know that was the subject of the ad and 'Blue' indicates that I might have had an image there that was blue as opposed to another colour.

If you are running Pay Per Click campaigns for your business (if you're not, you should), this is absolutely vital! It's not new technology but it is very surprising how many systems don't allow you do do this.

INTEGRATING YOUR WEBSITE
USING OUR API

Geek alert! For those of you that don't know, an API is some code which allows two web-based systems to talk to each other.

We have written an API that allows your website or landing page to input the details of an enquiry directly into your Business Automation System with a set of defaults. For instance, let's say you want the 'Lead Source' to be 'Website Enquiry' and to capture the tracking code, that's all easy.

Unlike most online web apps, if you're trying to integrate with our API, we'll help you do it. You're not just on your own so get in touch, let us know what you're trying to do and we'll advise the best way to go about it.

IF YOU ARE USING THE TRIAL

Capturing enquiries into your Business Automation System may not seem like a huge deal, but once you start you'll understand just how valuable it is. It's something we'll set up for you free if you're taking part in the Business Automation System Trial. Get in

Chapter 5

Email marketing In The Year We Actually Live In

BENEFITS OF
EMAIL MARKETING

If you've read my first book, Automate Your Business, you'll know I'm a huge advocate for using email marketing. It's the easiest and most effective way of moving prospects along your sales timeline, educating them and getting them closer to buying while giving them massive value in the process in a way that is scalable.

You'll no doubt have seen articles saying "Email Marketing is Dead". Possibly, but I'd suggest it's more to do with the fact that most people haven't evolved their efforts. Look at it this way, by the same token, direct mail has been "dead for years" according to most, but you're holding a book which I've posted to you. That's direct mail and by virtue of the fact that you have it in your hand, it's pretty clear it works all the time you're sending massive value.

The complaint really is that people can no longer spam offers 5x a week and make endless sales. The game has changed and the new version is to send MASSIVE GENUINE VALUE and almost guilt people into buying from you. I don't mean that in a negative way but in a "These guys have helped so much over the YEARS of course I'll buy from them, not anyone else" way.

Of course you want to be sending offers but keep it to an 80% value and 20% sales ratio if you can. Different industries will struggle to some extent but if you're a Lawyer, PR person, Marketer, Web Designer, IT guy or Business Consultant then you'll have no problem! You have endless content, tips and advice to share. Even if you run a sign company or you are a printer, what about sharing 10 really cool business card designs or some of the latest signs you've created, in a way that says "You could have something like this".

Email Marketing is one of those mediums that just needs to be used properly for it to work. If you use it like it's 2001 and assume 80% open rates then you'll always be disappointed. As Gary Vaynerchuk said recently, "Market in the year we actually live in". The guy has a point.

HOW TO DECIDE WHO TO SEND TO

Gone are the days where you can just send the same email to all your contacts, clients and enquiries and expect them all to equally care. How can every one of them need to hear the exact same message in the exact same context? I suggest doing micro emailing, whereby you'll send a super targeted email to a small sub-set of your list.

Let's say for instance you want to make a few quick sales. Who are the most likely people to buy from you? Existing clients that haven't bought for, say 6 months? If you hit them with an offer, it's highly likely you'll make sales. How about emailing an offer to all current sales enquiries that have outstanding quotes to progress their order faster. For example, "Place your order before Friday 4pm and we'll knock 10% off!".

Depending on the product or service you offer, you'll have different criteria to build your list from. Here are some of the different criteria you can create lists from in the Business Automation System. Make sure whatever system you use allows you to create similar lists and doesn't force you to do it manually.

- All enquiries, clients or contacts
- Grade (green, yellow or red)
- Lead Source (e.g. all website enquiries, all people you met at a trade show, everyone from a certain marketing campaign)
- Product - "Show me everyone that's had product X but not product Y"
- Haven't bought for - 1 month, 3 months, 6 months, 1 year or 2 years.

In fairness, most CRM systems allow some sort of search criteria; it's what happens once you have your people that is the issue. In our system, the next step is designing your email and choosing when to send. If the CRM system you're looking at or using doesn't integrate with your email marketing platform then you'll have to export the data, import it into the system then think about designing your email.

Remember, the idea of business automation is to be as efficient as possible. Anything that "cuts out minutes" from a process is worth investing money in.

INTRODUCING
MAILCHIMP

Fortunately, MailChimp, one of the leading Email Marketing platforms, has a free plan for up to 2000 contacts which is perfectly suitable for most small businesses. If you do cross over into their paid account, it's super cheap and you'll be doing well enough to justify the cost anyway.

You can create your free account here:
http://www.advantixgroup.com/links/mailchimp

One of the biggest complaints I hear about any email marketing platform these days is how many options and settings there are, most of which make no sense to the average user trying to send a basic campaign. This is why we have integrated MailChimp into the Business Automation System so you can not only produce highly targeted campaigns from your list of enquiries, clients and contacts, but the building and sending of your email takes minutes not hours.

Not taking part in the trial? Don't worry - this is still a great chapter and will let you know exactly how to create a great campaign with whatever email marketing platform you choose to use.

ANATOMY OF A GREAT
EMAIL MARKETING CAMPAIGN

The first thing to remember is to keep your email single focus. It's better to send 3 emails about 3 different things than send 1 about 3 different subjects. All great emails follow a simple formula.

- Sent through a reputable email marketing platform (Example: MailChimp).
- Professional looking design which matches your brand.
- Big, bold, attention-grabbing headline.
- A short, to the point message detailing exactly what the reader will get if/when they take action.
- A benefit driven call to action.
- Legalities like unsubscribe, business address etc.

If you are using the Business Automation System, it'll be integrated with your MailChimp account and the only things you need to concern yourself with are the headline, message and call to action. We've designed it so you can literally type and go.

To spice things up, it's worth adding in an image to excite the reader. If your product or service is photo friendly and you have plenty of imagery - great! If you're a consultant or something similar then you may want to check out Canva. It's a free website that lets you create beautiful imagery even if you have absolutely no design ability.
http://www.advantixgroup.com/links/canva

DESIGNING YOUR CALL TO ACTION

As we've established, every email campaign where you want any sort of action taken requires a "call to action". This is where you write, in a simple and easy to understand statement what you want the reader to do next. Some examples:

Bad: "Contact us for more information"
Good: "Click the green button below to download our PDF brochure instantly"

Bad: "Complete the form below to register your interest"
Good: "Fill in your details below to arrange a call with one of our expert advisors where you'll benefit from a free review of your portfolio"

CHOOSING WHEN TO SEND YOUR EMAIL

I covered this comprehensively in my last book, 'Automate Your Business' but I'll recap so you don't need to put this book down.

Think about who you are sending to. If you're sending to business owners, don't send them emails at 9pm expecting any sort of attention; the guy is probably eating dinner or chilling out watching TV. Send that same email at

3pm and you've got a fighting chance of it being read. On the other hand, if you're selling to consumers, sending an email at 8pm or 9pm might be a pretty good strategy.

Now we have the basics out of the way, here are some things I've found over the years while using email as my primary way of generating enquiries and sales:

Keep emails short
The shorter you keep your emails, the better. John Warrillow, author of 'Built To Sell', sends 1 line emails. Here's his recent email in it's entirety:

Subject: "Do you dream of getting an offer from a big, strategic acquirer?"
Body: "Here are five ways to make that dream a reality.".

That's it. His subject line is actually longer than his email. I would imagine his clickthrough rates are reasonably high with a thought-provoking question, then literally a link. It's an extreme method but if you're sending information and want people on your site, maybe it's not a bad strategy?

On the slightly more normal side of the fence, just keep it no longer than 3 paragraphs. No daunting looking walls of text.

Info in the morning
In the mornings we want to consume information, so if you're sending articles, ebooks or things for people to consume, do it in the morning. By morning, I mean 11am. Do not send earlier as people are busy. At around 11am, people start chilling out, having a coffee, and building towards lunch. That's a good time to send information.

Action in the afternoon

After lunch, people are a little more up-beat and ready to get things done and are more likely to 'do stuff' from emails you send. If you want someone to take any form of action, make sure you send these emails in the afternoon. I like to shoot for 3pm but certainly don't send any later than 4pm as the end of the work day starts creeping in and things get pushed to the next day. Of course, that would be fine if "tomorrow" didn't bring a new set of issues, things to do and distractions.

IF YOU ARE USING THE TRIAL

1. Select the people you want to email
2. Write headline
3. Write copy and insert imagery
4. Add a button (choose a colour that stands out against your brand and the link you want it to go to)
5. Schedule at a good time depending on your audience and what you want them to do. touch to arrange for it to be set up.

Chapter 6

Selling Like A Champion

RE-THINKING
QUOTES

Every business is a funnel. I'm sure you've heard the term 'sales funnel' before? If the aim is to make as much money as possible, we want to increase the conversion rate, or the number of people who buy. Those are the easiest and fastest ways to increase revenues.

When you quote someone, what are you really doing? You're saying "Would you like to buy X for £X?". Most businesses send something like this:

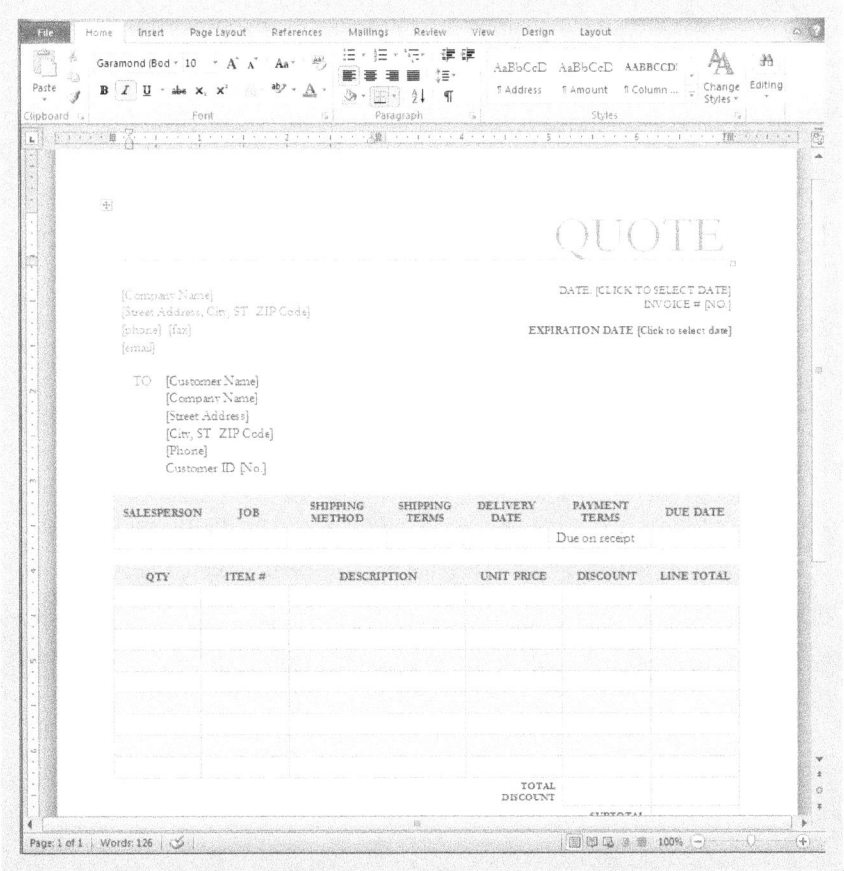

That is so disgusting, it's an insult to anyone who has to look at it!

If you are sending anything that looks anywhere near that bad then please please stop right this second, and take the action in this chapter to get it fixed immediately before you eat your next meal. That, or just start proactively sending your enquiries directly to your competition and save yourself the time building that quote in the first place. The end result is the same.

CREATING AN EPIC SALES PROCESS

There are 3 elements:

1. Electronically storing the details of the quotes. This starts by capturing enquiries from your website.
2. Sending a nice, professionally designed proposal.
3. Eliminating unnecessary steps.

1. Electronically storing the details

In my experience, I've seen various different ways of organising quotes you've sent. Some businesses use a basic CRM system which keeps all the details together; other businesses most commonly use an Excel spreadsheet, and scarily enough some don't document this at all.

The Business Automation System keeps track of all the quotes and proposals you send, when they're due to be followed up with and more. Whatever system you use, make sure it doesn't let you miss any opportunities that should be followed up with.

I would heavily avoid using spreadsheets at all costs. They are the death of all things automation and there's little use for them other than to produce pretty graphs. Another killer mistake is thinking, because you are excited about closing a certain deal, that you'll remember to follow up when you are supposed to. Everything needs to be documented or you'll forget it. You can not scale your business up, delegate and automate anything if it's stuck in your poor brain.

2. Sending Professionally Designed Proposals

I've never understood why so many businesses don't send professional looking proposals, instead of these horrific looking Microsoft Word "Quote Templates". They are horrible, unprofessional and do not inspire any level of confidence.

The way I see it, you have two choices. The first is to use a designer to professionally design a PDF which contains all the general information about your company, then attach an editable PDF with the costs and other specifics about the quote. The downsides to this are that it is completely untrackable, and PDFs are notoriously recognised as spam, so are immediately sent to most people's junk folders, and you'll have no idea if they even received your email.

Alternatively, you can send something web based rather than a PDF, so the look is consistent. There are two services, one called Quote Roller and another called Proposable which allow you to do just this but I found the look and feel of both to be very weak, so we made our own built into the Business Automation System. Proposals we send look like this:

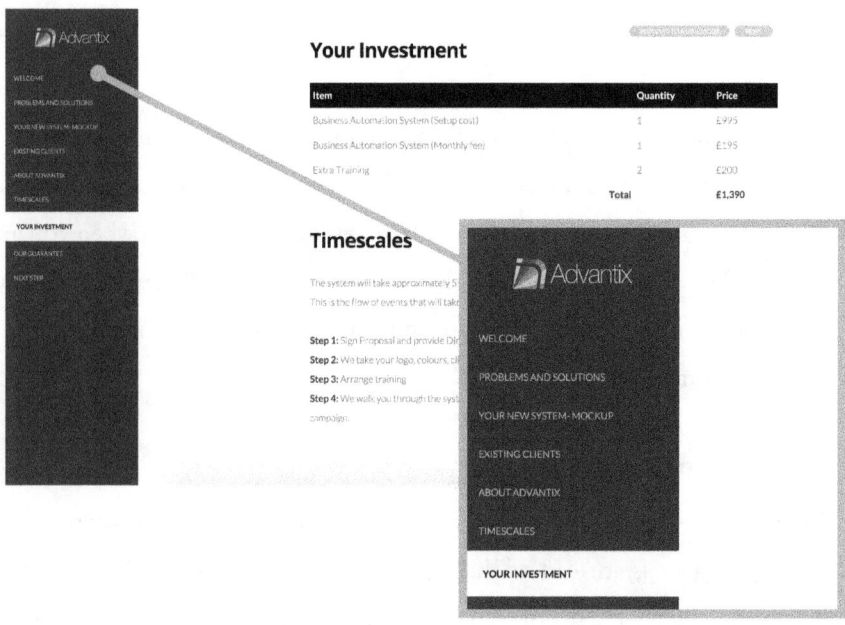

Branded in your logo and colours, clean, and best of all - trackable.

One of the biggest frustrations we have heard from business owners and sales people about sending proposals, is not knowing what happens after pressing send. They have no idea if the prospect got their email, looked at the price and closed it, spent 30 minutes reading every word or anything in between. If you're looking to follow up effectively and win more business, then knowing when someone opened your proposal, what they looked at and for how long is critical information. Here's how it looks:

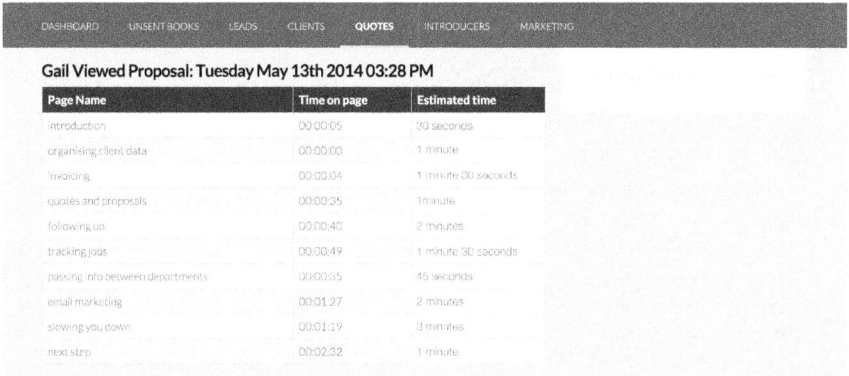

I would love to tell you that there are many other systems out there that do this and you can take your pick but there's a very good reason why we built our own. We just couldn't find anything very good.

3. Eliminating Unnecessary Steps

Another issue preventing businesses closing more deals is that they make their prospects jump through so many pointless hoops.

An old client of ours, let's call them Dimpene, sold financial products. Here was their sales process:
- They would make their potential client fill out an initial form to capture their details.
- Then before they'd talk to them, the prospect would have to sign an NDA and a non-circumvention agreement.
- Then they'd need to sign an engagement letter if they wanted to go ahead.
- As if that wasn't bad enough, the poor chap would have to go through almost exactly the same thing with the finance company they were being referred to.

Unsurprisingly, they're finding it a challenge converting sales enquiries.

YOUR NEW
SALES PROCESS

Your sales process should be no more complicated than this:

1. Have a conversation and extract all the information you need to produce a quote.
2. Send a proposal with your terms and conditions attached with the ability to sign it online.
3. Follow up at exactly the right time and ask for the sale.

SPEED UP YOUR SALES PROCESS
BY USING DIGITAL SIGNATURES

Every single business that doesn't literally accept cash over a counter should be utilising digital signatures as a way to speed up their sales process. It's more secure, legally certified and faster than old-fashioned signatures. It might seem like a foreign concept but any good quoting system should have the ability to sign online. I can't comment on other systems but the way our Online Proposal System works is simple:

1. You input the client's email address and send them the agreement from the system.
2. They click, read and type their name.

3. They're sent a 4 digit verification code to the email address that you provided.
4. They type the code in which verifies they are who they say they are.

It takes seconds for your clients to sign and speeds up the approval process from weeks to minutes. There are other services that do this like Docusign and EchoSign but they're separate to the system you'd use to send your proposal so it's an additional and unnecessary step for you and your client.

Investigate how you can implement this into your business.

WRITING AN IRRESISTIBLE BUSINESS PROPOSAL

Of everything in this book, this is going to take the most work but it is easily going to be the thing that makes the biggest difference to the number of prospects that say 'Yes'. A book that would be well worth reading is 'your Utterly Seductive Proposal' by Tim Coe. It's a walkthrough on how to position your company, to demonstrate its uniqueness at the front and centre of your marketing and sales efforts.

I've created a Proposal template as a Word Document which you can download. If you are trying the Business Automation System, you'll find a template ready to go in the Quotes section.

Download the Template:
http://www.advantixgroup.com/downloads/proposal-template

Here's how to write yours:

The Summary

Any proposal which has an "Our suggestion" or "What we're going to do" section which is longer than 3 pages, needs a summary. It should be short, to the point and someone should be able to skim read it and get the point within 60 seconds. Bullet points, bolding and short sentences and paragraphs are your friends here.

Assume that all someone is going to read is this part and the price.

What You're Going To Do

This is "the proposal" in essence. This is where you explain what you're going to do and the end result for the client. Do this in as much detail as is needed but not too much. Focus on the benefits and remember, they don't need to know HOW you do anything. State what you're going to do and what the benefits are for them.

People skim read these sections, I can tell you this for a fact because in our Online Proposal System, I can see exactly how long people are reading these these pages for.

Why We're Different and The About Us Page

It's worth thinking about what your business does differently to your competition. Perhaps think of things that your competition are famous for doing badly. For example, Virgin Media and their terrible customer service. If you offer the same service, but explain how your customer service is different and better, you win. A nice list of 6 things here is a sweet spot. Too many and it's unrealistic, too few and it doesn't look amazing.

The aim with the About page is to simply let someone know a few things they didn't know already. For example, awards you've won, major clients you've worked with, charities you support. Another reason for this page is to get someone who doesn't know you up to speed on what you're about.

Timescales

There are 3 main things people consider when buying something:

1. Can they do what I need?
2. Can they do it within my budget?
3. Can they do it in the timeframe that I need?

Hopefully you would have already established this on the phone or in person beforehand but it's certainly important to put it clearly in the proposal. I've done 6 steps as an example but you can add or remove some. The idea here is just to make the client feel comfortable while giving them a clear answer as to when they'll receive their product or service.

Investment

You could call this page Quote, Price, Costs or any other obvious phrase but I prefer 'Investment'. Anything that involves improving a current situation, coaching or training, software, web or marketing services or professional services is an investment. 'Costs' or 'Quote', to me cheapens what you're selling. It does need to make sense and be sensible though. A builder using the term investment would be silly if he was building a wall; but a loft conversion which would improve the value of the property? That's an investment in the truest sense of the word.

Be clear here about your price, and if you have payment plan options available, let them know what they are. What are the payment terms? There should be no doubt about the amount payable, over what period, how often and by what method.

Guarantee

Every business should offer a guarantee. No question. What could yours be? The objective is to have the reader thinking "I either get what I am paying for or not only do I get my money back but I also get _____".

The iPad example I've used in the Proposal Template is a bit of a joke but it does demonstrate the point. Giving something as a "sorry" for not doing a good job is the basis of a brilliant guarantee. What people often do is say they'll "redo it until it's right". This isn't anywhere near as good as the client can't get away from you if it all goes wrong.

Examples

It's vital that you include previous examples of you doing a great job. It shocks me beyond belief to see that some businesses provide no evidence that they can do what they're promising. A simple formula is this:

- What you did (A few word summary as a title)
- Brief description (A paragraph)
- Evidence (Photo, video, before and after pictures, a graph)
- Testimonial

If you don't have these things at hand easily you really should look to get them together and build up a collection each time you do a job, so your proposals are always fresh, current and interesting.

Next Step

Just explain the next steps. Don't explain the entire process, just the next few steps. Keep it simple and easy to understand.

Add a final "call to action" summarising in 2-3 sentences why you are the best choice. An easy way to lay this out is 3 simple statements:

- What you're going to do
- The main benefit
- Your guarantee

Example:

"You'll have a single Business Automation System running all your business processes. You'll be able to work less, earn more, while enjoying a simpler life. Try it for a full 3 months with our full support without paying a penny"

IF YOU ARE USING THE TRIAL

When you start using the Business Automation System you'll see we've already created a template for you. As part of starting a trial, we'll work with you to create the perfect proposal based on the products you sell, the service you provide and the benefits to your prospects.

FOLLOW UP WITH ENQUIRIES
LIKE GORDON GEKKO

Following up with sales enquiries is the task we wish we all did more of but never have the time for. We know how effective it is and we certainly appreciate it when people do it to us, so why do we find it so hard?

I know that in our business I used to be the world's worst at following up with people I'd sent a proposal to. I conducted some research amongst some of our clients and I certainly wasn't alone, so I dug deeper. Here's what I found:

- They were certain they'd make more money if they followed up more.
- They didn't because they didn't have the time.
- The reason they didn't have the time was because they felt each email needed to be written from scratch.
- They had no quick way of reminding themselves to contact the person.

So a follow up system that pre-empts what you want to say, reminds you when to do it and takes almost no time would be a pretty good start! We looked around and found nothing that solved all these issues at once, so we decided to make something ourselves and start using it internally.

Immediately I noticed that I was being reminded to contact people that I knew I had completely forgotten about. This happened again and again so I knew we were on to something. We called it Personal Touch.

CREATING YOUR OWN FOLLOW UP SYSTEM

For those of you using the Business Automation System Trial, Personal Touch is already built-in and ready to use. We've created some templates for you which you can use or amend as you see fit after reading this section.

Different Sequences

Depending on your sales process, you'll need different sequences to cater for the different stages your enquiries can be at. We use four:

1. Pre-Proposal - Designed to get people interested after reading a book.
2. Post-Proposal - Getting them to start the trial after knowing the price.
3. On-Boarding - Encourages them to use the system.
4. Become a Client - Guides them towards becoming a paying client.

My suggestion is to just focus on implementing one follow up sequence to start with. I would choose between Pre-Proposal and Post-Proposal. To find out which one you would benefit from the most, just look at the biggest drop off rate in your sales process. If most people you speak to want a proposal, then that area of your business doesn't have much of an issue and you should focus on Post-Proposal to increase conversion. If on the other hand your conversion rate is fairly good but you could do with sending more proposals, then focus on a Pre-Proposal sequence.

What to Say and When to Say it?

This completely depends on your business, what you sell, how you sell it and a million other factors but I can tell you that you already have a near perfect working template, you just aren't using it.

Go through your inbox and sent items and find the last sale you made where you had to chase. Look at the emails you sent and mark out the key ones where you were pro-active. Those are the emails that are going to make up the content. Also, look at the timing of the emails you sent and that will dictate the time delay between each communication. Were you leaving it quite a long time between emails? Be honest with yourself, could you maybe have sped up the process by being a little more aggressive in terms of timing?

Reminders

Where Personal Touch in the Business Automation System really comes into its own is the reminder portion. Every morning at 6am it will scan the system for any follow up emails that need to be sent that day and will present them on your Dashboard. You can open and send each one with 2 clicks making it lightning fast. Once you've done each one, it vanishes until they're all gone. It's this pro-active, daily prompting system that makes this so powerful.

Here's what it looks like:

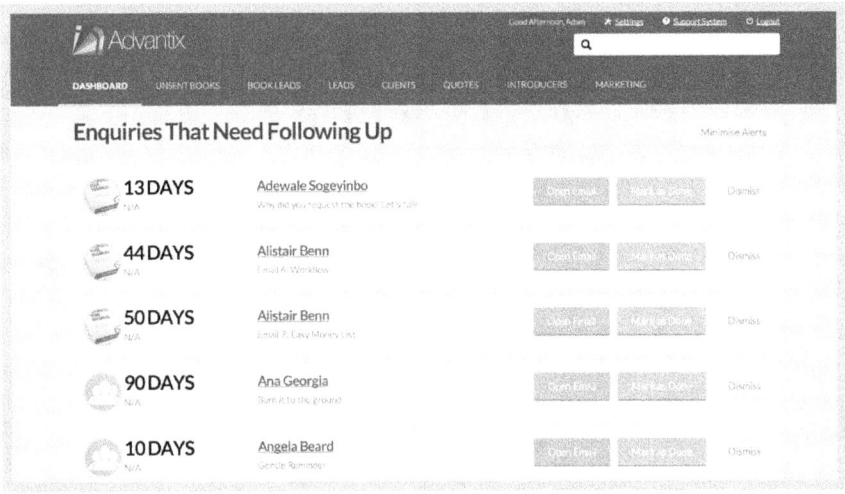

As much as I've tried to replicate it with Google Calendar or fancy spreadsheets, it just doesn't compare. That said, I realise not everyone reading this book will either want, or have the requirement for our system so I have made a spreadsheet which you can download below. It has some sample messages, the timing and a little marker for who's received which email. If you have a small number of sales enquiries and clients and you are good at keeping spreadsheets up to date then it'll be fine. Ask yourself this though, if you are forgetting to follow up, are you going to remember to update this spreadsheet?

Follow Up System Spreadsheet:

http://www.advantixgroup.com/downloads/followup-spreadsheet

Chapter 7

Simplifying Your Work Day

SPOTTING
THE ISSUES

When you win a job, if there's less of a process and more of a chaotic disaster, the likes of which wouldn't be uncommon at an unsanctioned rave, you might want to pay attention to this chapter.

There should be a very clearly defined workflow process that is documented and understood by everyone in the business. It's the one area of your business that you are trying to repeat as much as possible so it should be as slick and as streamlined as it can be. The way you do this is by focusing on merging, eliminating, outsourcing or automating as many tasks as possible. Here's our process:

No matter what happens, every single business that wants to use our software goes through that process. We have internal documentation for each stage and at any moment in time we know what needs doing and who should be doing it. If you do custom work for your clients, you might not be able to make it this simple but there should still be some sort of process.

In my last book, I went into great detail about how to define your processes. I still stand by everything I wrote in Automate Your Business on the idea of automating your workflow but I have refined my thinking on it somewhat.

If you want to read Automate Your Business, download it free here: http://www.advantixgroup.com/pdf/AutomateYourBusiness2014.pdf

DEFINING YOUR EXISTING WORKFLOW

If you're going to start re-hashing your existing workflow, start by writing down what it currently is. Don't sugarcoat it and pretend to yourself it's better than it is. Be truthful with yourself. There are four ways to shorten a process:

- Merging
- Eliminating
- Outsourcing
- Automating

Only once you've defined your workflow can you begin to think about whether it's possible to merge, eliminate, outsource or automate certain steps.

WRITE DOWN YOUR WORKFLOW
AS IT EXISTS NOW

MERGING, ELIMINATING, OUTSOURCING AND AUTOMATING

Merging:

The idea here is to kill two birds with one stone. If you have processes that either involve the same information but different people, or different information to be sent to the same person, you can merge these steps so long as they are consecutive. It's no good passing an instruction to someone that they don't need to action for 3 weeks.

The best example of merging is when you complete a task to progress the job and also want to email the client and let them know. This can and should be done at the same time. It makes your customer service consistent, professional and provides comfort to your clients which will result in making it considerably easier to get referrals.

Eliminating:

It's surprising how many stages of a process actually don't need to be done. You need to be ruthless. If you find yourself doing something that takes ages and produces further issues, stop doing it. Key culprits here are meetings and phone calls. I'm far from suggesting never meeting your clients and avoiding calls but if you replaced "I just wanted to give you an update" calls to emails and saved calls for discussions, how much time would you save over a month?

Outsourcing:

There's no escaping it. You'll need to outsource as much of your business as you can. Chris Howard once said "Never outsource your core competency". He's right, but most businesses don't understand what their core competency actually is. For us, it's not developing software, it's marketing and writing. If I were to outsource that, I'd be stupid as that is the core of what makes us different. Software Development is a commodity and any trained developer can do it with the right plan.

One of the top directors at McDonalds once said "We sell hamburgers but we're in the Real Estate business". You wouldn't think of McDonalds as a property company but that's exactly what they are.

Think about your business and what you produce. Is the actual thing you sell really something that only you can do? If you are a consultant then maybe you can't outsource the part that involves your thinking, but if you have back-end work that needs doing, you should be looking to outsource that element. Even if you are a consultant, is there any reason why you couldn't have junior consultants following the documentation, training and responses that you've already produced? If you did that, could you not charge considerably more for your services? It's worth a thought.

Automation:

The only way to automate a manual process is by doing work upfront and using digital communication to handle the delivery. You can't get software to build a house or mend a boat engine, but you can automate pre-written emails and create a set of standard communication for the admin portion of your process. If your production is manual in any way, you can't truly automate, but you can merge and eliminate as much as possible.

Trim the Fat:

Now I want you to go back through your existing workflow process.
- Put a line through any steps that are being eliminated entirely.
- Use an arrow to connect two that are being merged.
- Put a star next to the ones that are being outsourced.
- If you're going to automate, write out your new process from scratch.

ACTION YOUR CHANGES

On the next page, write out your new workflow. Take the merging, eliminating, outsourcing and automating into account. This will serve as the backbone of your business. You can print this out, stick it on the wall and get everyone working from it. If you are using the Business Automation System Trial you can set this up in the system itself so every job you do will operate from the same process.

Some businesses might have a different workflow for each product. For instance, the process for making a table is different to making a chair. For every product you set up in the Business Automation System, there's a corresponding workflow for it.

YOUR NEW
WORKFLOW

CREATING A
COMMUNICATION TIMELINE

The key differentiator between good customer service and bad customer service is the communication. If you communicate well, clearly, frequently and honestly, you'll please your clients every single time. If you don't, you'll do alright but you'll likely get a lot more phone calls asking how jobs are coming along. Your referrals will be considerably lower and the loyalty will be almost non existent because your clients won't feel looked after.

Great customer service is mostly just being a nice person, so seeing as most of us are nice people, why do so many companies dish out devastatingly terrible experiences to their clients? The answer is 'time'. When you have to choose between replying to a client about something which you know is being taken care of, or finishing a proposal for the new client, the proposal wins every time.

That said, while some things like writing proposals require the personal touch, you can automate the bulk of your communication so at least there's a consistent message being delivered that doesn't take any time to send. Think of it as great customer service by just doing your job.

Everything I'm talking about here is all part of the Business Automation System. For those that aren't taking part in the Trial, there are some really great project management tools out there like Basecamp, which we use for big custom projects. There's also Trello which I've heard is worth a look too.

Chapter 8

Automating Your Business Finances

THE IDEAL
REVENUE MODEL

In an ideal world, your business would sell a product or service that can be delivered either completely by staff, by outsourcing or digitally. I want you to think about ways your business can charge a monthly fee, either in addition to, or instead of a one off fee.

A classic example of this is Hove based accountants, Bainbridge Lewis (www.bainbridgelewis.co.uk). They could charge an annual fee like most accountants, but instead they take the entire annual fee and split it over the year into monthly payments. This makes cashflow far easier to manage as you don't end up with fluctuating months of good and bad income. In addition, it's much easier to predict business growth.

Consider how you are billed by most other firms; Your website, your office rent, bills, utilities - they're all monthly. If it's even remotely conceivable that you can attach a monthly cost to your service then you should give it some serious thought. If you don't want to re-think your pricing model, then how about creating a new product entirely to cater for it? You will be putting yourself in good stead to deal with any dip in sales in the future and really solidify the business. In John Warrillow's book, 'Built To Sell', he talks about the idea of building your business as if you are trying to sell it even if you don't have any intention of doing so.

A good example of this is my brother Rob's business. He runs a video production company called Silver Lining Productions. They create amazing short films which tell the stories of their clients' businesses in creative ways.

Rob sat down with Tim Coe, the USP Pro to create his Utterly Seductive Proposal and what they found was that Rob's business could be built around weekly distributed videos, filmed in bulk, that build an audience for his clients. They called it YouTube Weekly (www.youtube-weekly.com). This service has a £495 monthly fee for shooting in 1 session then they edit the videos and distribute them over the month.

At the moment, Rob works with each of his clients privately but he could easily bring in an editor to do that portion, or a camera man depending on whether he preferred shooting or editing. It's a fantastic shift from being a required part of the job, to selling an end result which is repeatable.

You can do the same sort of thing. Want another example? Socks? Boxer shorts? Condoms? You don't think you can turn those into a monthly revenue model? Of course you can. Manpacks.com created a business that sends you a monthly supply of a range of different mens' items for a fixed monthly fee.

Just keep it in the back of your mind and consider how you could turn what you do into a monthly revenue model. If you are stuck for ideas, make an appointment and put me on the spot and challenge me.

THE PROCESS
OF SENDING INVOICES

When you invoice your clients, it's likely you're either using Microsoft Word or some form of accounting software. If it's Microsoft Word, please, please stop. It's highly embarrassing for everyone. Let me explain why:

1. You have no automatic record of invoicing.
2. A list of all outstanding invoices is hard to produce.
3. Automating reminders for unpaid invoices is impossible.
4. Your invoices probably don't look great.
5. They take time to produce, open the previous one, click save-as, change the details.
6. The whole operation doesn't look or feel professional in any way shape or form.

Simply put, invoicing via Microsoft Word is a terrible thing to do and you should change this, but what to?

My personal recommendation is Xero. It's by far the best online accounting software in existence. Invoicing takes seconds, setting up repeat invoices is a doddle and more importantly, you can see at a glance how much money you're owed and by who. What's more, they have an iPhone and Android app, meaning you can invoice at any time.

They have a free trial, sign up here:

http://www.advantixgroup.com/links/xero

THE TIMING
OF SENDING INVOICES

Invoicing promptly is one of the easiest things you can do to increase cashflow. A friend of mine joined a firm who are now a client and one of the first things she did was put prompt invoicing in place. The average number of days from invoice date to payment was 140. She brought it down to 24. On a turnover of £3,000,000 a year, that's a lot of money not in your bank account that should be.

Work out the moment you should be invoicing and build it directly into your workflow. Even invoicing a day or two late can have a huge impact on cashflow, and for any business - cashflow is king. What most business owners do from my experience is wait until they have enough invoicing to do, then send several at once. In a corporate environment you just want to get your invoice in as soon as possible because it's a time thing. In a small business, the timing of when you invoice can be huge!

Imagine you run a flooring company and your client has just come home and had the "Wow!" factor seeing their brand new floor; then 1 hour later the invoice comes through marked "Please pay within 7 days". It's very likely they'll pay it right there and then. What about if you leave it a few days then invoice? The excitement has worn off somewhat, and now life has got in the way which could delay payment.

It's a hypothetical situation but a completely possible one. One thing is true though - invoice promptly and you'll be paid far quicker.

30 DAY INVOICES ARE BULL****

You've completed a job, here's an invoice for the balance which says you have 30 days to pay. Why? Who started this ridiculous trend of giving people a full month, or longer to pay. My brother Rob for his first job, as funny as it is, put "Please pay within 1 hour of receiving this invoice" as the payment terms. That was it - 1 hour. You want to know what happened? They paid in 25 minutes! Call it ridiculous but it worked. We issue 7 day invoices and can't see any reason to wait longer. You should do the same.

METHODS OF ACCEPTING PAYMENTS

I've gone over this in my previous book so I'll just give you the headlines. Do not accept cheques under any circumstances. Standing orders should only be accepted if the amount is big enough that you would notice if it was cancelled.

I would suggest that if you are going to have standing orders come in, just set a repeating reminder in your calendar system for a few days after the standing order date (to account for Bank Holidays and Weekends) and simply check that way. Having a simple knowledge of a client's monthly payment date is a great idea. You can store this in your Business Automation System or any good CRM.

Accepting cash in my opinion is silly:

- You get charged to cash it.
- It's a risk to walk it to the bank.
- It takes time and last time I checked, you can't cash it if you're on a beach in Maui.

Stick to digital money. Use services like:

Square - http://www.advantixgroup.com/links/square
iZettle - http://www.advantixgroup.com/links/izettle

They allow you to accept card payments anywhere, directly from your phone or tablet. A superb cash replacement. If you really want to accept cash, offer a small discount for digital payments.

If you're getting on-board with the monthly payment model, one method of accepting payments that you can't ignore is Direct Debit. As someone whose business is 100% based on monthly fees, I can tell you that starting to accept Direct Debit was one of the best business decisions I've ever made. It makes up-selling so easy, all the money comes in at once and if there are any issues you are told about them instantly. For example, we had 1 failed report this morning which was a cancelled Direct Debit. They'd actually done this because they're switching accounts but it was simple to deal with. We got the notification, emailed the client to tell them and immediately they responded with the new account details. Without having a Direct Debit service it would have been weeks before we'd found out, then we'd have to chase the missing payment, everything would be out of sync and it would be a mini-disaster.

The two Direct Debit services I can recommend are:

Smart Debit - http://www.advantixgroup.com/links/smartdebit
Go Cardless - http://www.advantixgroup.com/links/gocardless

FIRE THE BOOKKEEPER
HIRE XERO

At a certain point, a bookkeeper is necessary, but what I want to challenge is the point at which you get one involved. My thinking is it's a lot further down the line than you might think. Usually, it's a pretty good deal. You'll pay around £15 an hour for someone to take all that nasty receipt entering off your hands. Bonus. But what if you never had that nasty receipt entering to begin with?

What if you could do your entire week's worth of bookkeeping in 20 minutes on your phone while sitting on the train? Coming back to the original point of this book about having systems do the work for you, Xero has done exactly that. Here's what happens:

You connect your Online Banking to Xero, and it pulls in your entire statement then starts automatically matching income with invoices you've raised, outgoings with regular expenses you've told it about before and simply asks the question "What's this?" a handful of times for the transactions it doesn't recognise. Over time it will learn your spending habits to the point where after just 4 months, our entire month's bookkeeping was taking 15-20 minutes. Because they also have a great iPhone and Android app, you can actually do your bank reconciliation wherever you like. It's a true step forward.

For this reason, I would suggest you'd need thousands and thousands of records per month (most of which would be automatically detected) before even thinking about getting a bookkeeper involved.

The idea of Business Automation really stems down to the core principle of using technology to its fullest extent, pushing it to the absolute limit and only using people where technology can't do the job.

This might seem daunting, but it doesn't have to be. The process I've laid out in this walkthrough, strikes the perfect balance between automating in small chunks, and giving you an ROI as quick as possible.

PART 3
DESIGNING YOUR NEW LIFE

Chapter 9

Making The Transition

GET YOUR SYSTEM
SET UP AND IN PLACE

By now, you'll know whether you are going to try using the Business Automation System or cobble together the alternative suggestions in this book to create a cocktail of systems from which to run your business.

If you are using multiple systems, my suggestion to you is setting aside some time in two stints. The first will be to find the systems you actually need and work out what information you need in order to get them usable. The second stint will be to actually import your data and set everything up. As much as business software companies these days love to promote instant set up, none of them truly offer it. This includes ours, which is why we do it for you.

THINGS TO CONSIDER WHEN
CHOOSING WEB BASED SOFTWARE

Time and Effort to set these systems up:

If you find a CRM system to sign up for, you are going to have to import or type in all of your clients' details. If you've found a quoting system, you'll have to put all your existing quotes and prospects into the system. These are massive tasks no matter how simple the system in question makes it. This is why doing this in two sessions is the best way to ensure you have everything you need. Bear in mind also that some systems require a credit card before signing up, so be sure to set reminders on the length of the free trial to avoid any charges.

Considering Service:

Each system is going to provide a different level of service. Think about where they are based. If you're in the UK and they're in San Francisco, USA and they provide "business hours" service, that means at best you'll only get 2 hours of support while they're working. Not ideal.

Some provide only email support, others provide phone support so you really need to weigh these things up and work out what is best for your business.

Costs:

Most systems for some reason punish you for having more staff and charge per user. Consider the immediate cost but also the potential future cost if you plan on growing your business. Other systems charge a transaction fee like GoCardless or a mix of monthly and transaction fees like SmartDebit. Once you've worked out the different systems you need and worked out a monthly cost for the total solution, only then can you start comparing apples to apples.

Integrations:

Do the systems you are looking at all go together? Do they talk to each other? When you're recording a quote in your CRM, does that then create a proposal in your proposal system or does it mean you have to manually copy from one system to another? Consider also that just because something says it integrates doesn't mean it'll do exactly what you need. Test both systems together and see how good it truly is.

If this is sounding like a Herculean task, that's because it is. Of course this is a slightly self serving suggestion but being as fair and reasonable as possible, we happily do all the setup of your Business Automation System if you want to try using our system first. If it turns out that it's not right for you, at least you've got all your data in one place and can start using other systems with minimal effort.

TAKE ONE DAY OUT THE OFFICE EVERY WEEK

Once you have your new system in place, you can start to scale back your working hours. A simple thing you can do to build the level of acclimation to you not being in the office, is scheduling 1 day per week out of the office. Take your phone and laptop and go somewhere inspiring. I usually go to the Seattle Hotel at Brighton Marina. It's a short drive from my house so it's not much of an inconvenience, but still far enough to keep me away from where I usually work. The benefits are massive!

To start with, the mere fact that you're out of your usual working environment is naturally inspiring and it gets your brain thinking in different ways. You'll become used to dealing with issues with just digital devices and not hordes of paper work. You'll stop scribbling notes down on a sheet of paper which happens to be sitting on your desk, and instead make notes against the client in your Business Automation System.

You'll plan your day by the tasks assigned to you in your system and not by what's written on a whiteboard or worse yet, reacting to people randomly asking for favours in the office.

The reason I suggest 1 day per week is that it's completely achievable. It doesn't have to be out at a fancy hotel. If you usually go to the office, you can simply stay at home; just make sure you're not going to have family/pets/tv/games/gym distractions or the whole thing will be pointless. Once you've seen how productive 1 day per week is, you can increase it to suit your lifestyle.

PLANNING WHAT YOU WANT
FROM YOUR NEW LIFESTYLE

What do you want from your life? Usually in business books, the author is trying to get you to put the new information in the book through the filter of the goal that you've set yourself. For this reason, "goal setting" is usually right at the beginning. I wanted to take the opposite approach. The big grand "If I could have anything" goal for most people I speak to, is to work, take a £100,000 salary and work 40 hours a week. That's not bad but let's be real; if you really wanted to, you could probably get that anyway by taking a job elsewhere. I've left this section until now because I want you to see what's possible before thinking about what you can achieve yourself.

I think there are 3 types of goals you can set yourself here in relation to what this book can help you with:

- Money Goals
- Time Goals
- Activity Goals

Money Goals

It's a multi-step process but it's not very difficult to make more money when you've achieved what you already have, going about things in a less than ideal way. When you stop letting enquiries slip through the net, start sending world-class proposals and follow up like a champion, it's pretty clear you'll close more business. Compound that with your time being freed up to work on more marketing, and utilising email marketing to existing clients on a regular basis, and you have a pretty potent recipe for increasing revenues.

What's your number? What do you want to be earning per month? Forget the idea of leaving money in the business forever. You can't spend it when you're dead. Speak with your accountant and figure out the most tax-efficient way to extract cash on a monthly basis.

Lessons from Frank

Someone I've personally learned a lot from and you could too, is Frank Kern. In a really under watched but certainly not under appreciated speech, Frank takes a woman on-stage through writing out every material thing she could possibly want, then working out a monthly cost for it all. Then he asks a series of questions to work out how many visitors she needs to her website in order to have the life she wants. It's an incredibly brilliant, yet simple bit of maths.

I've always felt arbitrarily picking a number from thin air as a monthly income goal is pointless. It's not connected to anything meaningful and leaves you with no drive whatsoever.

Let's kick it off by listing everything you want. I've given you a head start by asking about typical material wants like cars and houses. There's space on the next page for you to fill in the blanks. For things like mortgages, just use a mortgage calculator to give an approximate monthly cost. If you need more space then use some paper to complete your list. Please don't let the space I've given you here dictate any sort of limit.

Once you've done that, add them up and that is the monthly income your business needs to generate you. Write it on the opposing page and cement that number into your brain.

COCKTAILS & PALM TREES

WHAT NICE THINGS
DO YOU WANT IN YOUR LIFE?

	1ST HOME	MONTHLY COST
	2ND HOME	MONTHLY COST
	DREAM CAR	MONTHLY COST
	TRAVELS	MONTHLY COST
	BOAT	MONTHLY COST
	SAVINGS	MONTHLY COST

THE MONTHLY INCOME
I NEED TO FUND MY LIFESTYLE IS…

Time Goals:

It's incredibly hard to want to work any less than a regular 40-hour week. It just seems normal, but why? Who decided that regardless of the profession, position, skill set or efficiency, everyone needed to work exactly a 40-hour week?

If you are buying a company, launching a product, writing a book, launching a huge marketing campaign then it's likely you'll be working your tail to the bone to complete tasks. I have weeks when I'm working literally every waking second. I have other weeks when I'll complete 7 or 8 hours of work. I used to feel guilty but recently I've come to accept that it's just how things should be.

Think about the middle of the summer when you want to chill out, play with your kids and jet off on random trips. Assuming everything's ticking over, do you really need to be working a pointless 40-hour week or are you better off attaching yourself to zip lines and launching yourself over 500ft drops on a Monday afternoon?

That's exactly what I did:

We're all wired differently. Personally, I like to keep things a little random. Mental desk-bound businessman one month; rave going, jet setting lunatic the next. For the less mental of you, you might just decide that you want to work a maximum of 15 hours in the business. That could be 15 hours of going into the office, working, making calls, doing email and general busy work. The rest of the time you are either going to be learning an instrument, enjoying dinner with your partner at a reasonable time or planning the growth of the business. Whatever the situation, the remainder of your week isn't dictated, it's your choice.

THE NUMBER OF HOURS
I WANT TO WORK IN A WEEK IS…

Activity Goals

Why do you have a business? Why do you even work? I mean, you could easily claim off the Government and sit at home all day doing nothing, so what is it you work for? Working for the sake of working is a pretty pointless thing to do. Maybe you want nice cars and houses, to go on lots of holidays or provide as well as possible for your family. These are all valid reasons to earn money but let's dig a little deeper.

Do you have a dormant passion that could be revived as a hobby? What about running a football team, getting back into sport yourself, getting back in the gym in a serious way? What are all the things you've not done because you've had the business and had no time?

What places have you always wanted to visit? What, if you had to, would you put on your bucket list right now? If you're struggling, I'll ask you the same question my friend Heidi asked me when I said "I have no bucket list". She said "So there's nothing that you could do now, but won't be able to in the future?" Actually yes, there was. I had always wanted to see the great Spanish International Football team play. The team that had won 2 European Championships back to back with a World Cup victory in the middle, and went into the 2014 World Cup as favourites. You might not be into football and that's fine, but I am and that was always something I wanted to do. So I booked a flight to Madrid two weeks later and saw Xavi, Iniesta and Casillas kick a ball around against a star-studded Italy.

Not only was it a masterclass performance and they won the game, but the city of Madrid was incredible! I took a call from a client while I was out there. It seemed a shame that we could both do our jobs from anywhere in the world, but he was stuck in an office in London while I was floating about on a lake in the middle of Madrid.

There's an Australian comedian that I have followed for years who had finally decided to play a string of shows over in the UK but was only playing the Edinburgh Fringe Festival. I'd never been to Scotland so booked a flight, got my ticket, jumped on AirBnB.com for a room and I'm on my way.

I once had a potential client call me while I was snowboarding. Not just while I was there, but literally while I was snowboarding down a slope. I assumed it was my cousin calling me from the other end of the mountain so I took the call without stopping and had a great, yet amusing chat while doing jumps in a board-park. He loved it and found it hilarious. What better example of our service can there possibly be than taking a call like that.

My goals are mostly travel related. I need almost zero excuse to visit a new city or country. I explained before, the reason I called this book Cocktails & Palm Trees is because I just wanted the financial and the time freedom to visit whatever places I like without worry. I believe massively in abundance. There's an abundance of potential clients and an abundance of money but I don't believe in an abundance of opportunity. Too many people think these things will last forever and the reality is, they don't.

Look at it like this - my friend spent many years putting off a 3 month trip of travelling round the world. He was saving up and planning every tiny little bit, but instead of just going he waited. Of course, there never is the perfect moment but he left it and left it; then he got a serious ear injury which essentially means he can't fly now. It's possible this will never get fixed and that trip will probably never happen for him.

Take your chances while you can. Before you think you can't take chances now, even if it doesn't seem perfect, it doesn't matter - just do it anyway.

I could go on and on but I think it's less about what I've done and what I want as a 29 year old single guy, and more about the things that you want at whatever age and stage in your life you are at.

Think about all these things and start writing them down on the next page. I also want you to write what the first step is if you wanted to do that activity. Let's say you want to get back in shape. The first thing might be to call a personal trainer, sign up to a weekly bootcamp or simply buy some weights. Whatever it is, write down the first step and easiest thing you can do to make it a reality.

We'll come back to this list shortly in the last chapter.

THE ACTIVITIES
I WANT TO DO ARE…

Chapter 10

Getting Your Team On-Board

GETTING YOUR TEAM
EXCITED ABOUT CHANGE

If you're a solo entrepreneur you can skip this chapter entirely, but it might make for useful reading if you are planning on hiring in the future.

In my years of putting systems into businesses and training their teams, I've seen many scenarios work brilliantly. At the same time I've been met with a few "What on earth is this?" expressions when I sit down to do the training, only to find out the Managing Director hasn't actually told the staff anything.

Here are the simplest ways to get your team on-board so everyone can be excited about your new system, not confused or annoyed.

LET THEM KNOW IN ADVANCE
IT'S FOR THEIR BENEFIT

I know what you're thinking, "I'm the boss, I'll just tell them this is how it's going to work and that's how it'll be". You can try but you'll find people hate change at the best of times, most of all at work and the last thing you need for morale is resistance.

In our experience of training people to use our systems, the best results come when the client has not only pre-warned the staff what's going on, but has actively involved them, so they are excited about the upcoming changes to their job.

The best thing you can do is continue to remind them that their jobs will become easier. If you ask your staff what their biggest complaints are about their job, they will probably tell you a lack of communication between departments, spelling mistakes causing issues and having to type information into multiple systems. When you can confidently tell them that 90%, if not 100%, of those issues will go away, it's amazing how quickly you'll get them on-side.

I will often meet with or interview key members of a team and ask them about their pain-points. At what stage does the process start to fall apart? At what point do they stop relying on copy and paste emails and have to actually do their craft? What systems have they put in place off their own back to speed things up?

The key is to empower your team to speak up about the efficiencies they have created and the issues they experience on a daily basis.

Improving the efficiency of your staff can make a huge difference to your bottom line. It's not uncommon for almost entire job roles to be automated or for a business to go from two admin staff to one. Let's say you have five staff including yourself, and our approach and systems save each staff member 15 minutes each day. That's it - just 15 minutes.

Lets do the maths.

15 minutes x 5 staff = 75 minutes per day saved

Multiply that by 250 working days in a year = 18,750 minutes (312 hours)

Assume an hourly rate of £10 per hour.

Saving of £3,120 per year or £8.56 per day.

Our system for instance costs much less than this.

I don't want you to think of these as inflated figures. If your staff only saved 15 minutes per day I'd be horrified. It's a beautiful realisation that you can not only grow your business without adding staff, but also scale down the staff count without affecting revenues or customer service, and dramatically increasing profitability.

WHAT IF THEY DON'T WANT TO LEARN A NEW SYSTEM?

Then you let them go. You can't be held hostage by your own staff. No one person, no matter how good they are is bigger than a company. Would Real Madrid survive without Cristiano Ronaldo? Of course it would be tricky in the short term but everyone else would pick up the slack, rise to the challenge and they would build new stars.

This is YOUR business. It's not a vehicle with which to employ people and give them whatever they want at your expense. Consider their views about HOW you are going to streamline their workflow but don't let them dictate to you and tell you it's not happening. If after doing this their job doesn't need doing anymore and you want to let them go because there's nothing for them to do - go for it. If you want to offer them another opportunity within the business perhaps in a marketing or sales based role then great, but you must do what's best for business.

ASSET
PROTECTION

Going forward, as I suggested at the beginning of this book, your focus should increasingly become geared towards marketing. Let me explain why…

A new client of ours, we'll call him Dan, had a business with a few partners and the business was split up so they could each go their own way. It's taken Dan a matter of days to set up new websites, re-do the marketing he'd done on Google Adwords and get ready to go again. Because the others didn't do the marketing for the business, they are now left with no idea how to generate enquiries from cold as that was Dan's job. Dan got the short straw in the business split but because of his skills and foresight to focus on the marketing part of the business, he's in a much better position than the others combined.

You can't unlearn marketing. It stays with you forever. You need to protect yourself against any kind of downturn, rogue staff, big clients leaving and any other random event that could bring your business down. The only way to do this is to learn the skill that brings any business out of a slump. Of course, once you become great at marketing, it's unlikely you'll have those issues to begin with. If you need convincing, how is it that Richard Branson can start hit business after hit business again and again? He knows marketing, he knows positioning and he's rarely wrong. Focus on learning this as a skill.

Chapter 11

The Big Jump and The £1,000 Reward

A QUICK
RECAP

So let's have a little recap. You've been walked through how to create incredible marketing, world class proposals, how to follow up like a champion and bring in more revenue. You've been taught how you can automate, or at least simplify your workflow and reduce your finance admin down to a few hours per month at worst. We've set some goals relating to the nice things you want, the hours you want to work and the activities you want to do.

What's next is to actually do it. I have a pretty big incentive for you if you choose to take me up on my challenge.

What is the one thing from our goal setting section that stood out that you really want to do more than anything? It should be an activity, a trip, a hobby. Something you could, with a push in the right direction and a little incentive, actually start to do right now.

Let's just say, that top of your list without question is wanting to buy a Cobra Rib, why not hire one for the day or weekend? What about writing a book? Open a notepad, jot down the things you'd include and start getting yourself excited!

My challenge to you is write your immediate goal from your list of activities in the box below, send me a picture of it to ads@advantixgroup.com or tweet me @AdamHempenstall.

Next, I want you to take a step towards actually doing it.

It might be something you can do over a weekend but I really want you to push yourself and get out the office during the week. What needs to happen for you to do this thing? Have someone take care of the phones? What about having someone look at your email and only call your mobile if it's urgent? What things are stopping you from putting this book down right now and going and doing whatever it is you want to do? Write down every potential issue that could crop up. Get them handled or dismiss them as a non-issue.

Here's the deal: You take me up on my challenge and take that bold step towards doing something epic, something you've always wanted to do and prove to me you've taken the step towards doing it. If you do, then decide to become a paying client, I'll give you £1,000 off whatever you choose to do with us.

So, are you going to accept my challenge?

So you've got my free book, you try our system out and make sure it adds value 10x what it costs. If it does and you want to become a full client, you start paying, less the £1,000 gift I'm giving you as a reward for taking action and living out a dream.

WHAT NEXT?

Hopefully by now you'll be ready to take me up on my challenge, you have yourself a Business Automation System Trial started and have booked your call with me so we can set your system up just how you need it.

If not, book your call here:

http://www.advantixgroup.com/book-call

If you've had a look at our videos and website and don't feel like our solution will help you, I hope you feel like this book has been of value. Hopefully I'll have opened your eyes to a better way of doing something which will in turn help you get closer to living the lifestyle you want.

As I'm sure you can appreciate, this world of technology, apps and business software is ever changing. Our clients don't need to worry themselves with it because we are the filter. Many new software companies get launched which look great but in reality are absolutely rubbish when we test them out. It's our job to filter it all for you. If you're not coming on board with us, that's completely cool but I would recommend you start to get yourself interested in this idea of business automation. Learn about it, read some blogs on how to streamline processes, use templates for repeatable tasks and get your business based in the cloud.

THE BEST INNOVATORS
NEVER STOP INNOVATING

Your work is never done when it comes to automating. There's always something that can be improved. Use the 80/20 principle all the time when assessing what needs attention, then move onto the next thing. Think about your business like your house, there must be a room which needs a fresh coat of paint? When that's done, it'll be something else and your business is exactly the same. Never stop innovating and thinking of new ideas. Keep your brain stimulated with new ideas from different sources.

I'm currently in Milan and there's a restaurant here which gives you an iPad when you walk in and you order directly from it. No order taking from the staff, no waiting around or trying to flag someone down. The place can be completely rammed and it still creates an element of calmness as the servers don't need to worry about taking orders and remembering stuff, they just need to bring the food to the right places. Very smart!

Keep thinking of ways you can improve, streamline and simplify your processes in order to make your business that much better.

LAST CALL:
ALL REMAINING AUTOMATORS

When it really comes down to it, the dust has settled, the smoke has cleared and all you are left with is yourself and your decisions, are you going to regret not doing everything you can to enjoy doing the things you love with the people you love?

Ultimately you could just sit around doing nothing and that's completely cool, but I'm pretty sure you can't do that and live the life you dream about. You've created a business that I'm imagining could be better organised, better automated and create you more free time. This is your chance to do it and we are here to help.

There are enough things to do to get everything sorted out, organised and implemented, the last thing you really need is to spend your valuable time trying to find a bunch of systems and cobble them together with the hope that it'll work. In a 20-30 minute phone interview, I'll personally be able to tell you exactly what systems you'll need, how best to go about automating, how long the process could take and give you enough ideas to melt your brain on creative ways to make you stand out in the process.

This has been my love, passion and life's work to create the systems we've made. Beyond that though, to figure out how to automate a business lightning quick, then put it into action.

Please, put me to the test. If you don't think it's possible to automate your business or live your "cocktails and palm trees" lifestyle, try me. If you think you've got it covered, great but have you really thought of everything? Let's see if our ideas match.

My goal with writing this book was to get the best ideas and tools into the hands of people that need them. This includes incredible systems like MailChimp, Xero and SmartDebit, as well as our own.

You're about to take on a mammoth task and I feel it's my job to make that as easy as possible for you. I know from experience exactly what you need to get started and lay that first brick. If you give these ideas a chance, I'll meet you half way.

Now you've had this book you'll get some emails which enhance the reading experience, remind you of things to try and it's also my outlet to give you more ideas which have evolved since printing this book. If at any point you don't like them or feel they aren't particularly valuable, just unsubscribe.

Call, email or text me with any questions you have, and I will do my absolute best to answer them and help you.

Thank you for reading and giving my ideas a chance. Please take the challenge, step up and start by getting yourself signed up to the Business Automation System. Then let's work together to make your "cocktails and palm trees" lifestyle a reality.

Take the next step:

www.advantixgroup.com/cocktailsandpalmtrees/trial

Hopefully we'll meet soon.

Your friend,

Adam Hempenstall

Email me on adam@advantixgroup.com
Tweet me @AdamHempenstall

www.ingramcontent.com/pod-product-compliance
Lightning Source LLC
Chambersburg PA
CBHW072214170526
45158CB00002BA/602